MW00487585

"Rob Saler amazingly moves the discussion of sabbatical beyond its initial roots that focus on the pastor to the next stage of maturity where, by the grace and mercy of God, both pastor and people are renewed and shape a new season of shared ministry together. A must read for pastors and leaders of congregations!"

— Frank A. Thomas, Christian Theological Seminary, Indianapolis

"If your congregation is considering a pastoral sabbatical, this book is your companion to create an extraordinary experience for both clergy and congregation. With clarity and winsome examples, Robert Saler provides practical wisdom on how to shape a sabbatical in which clergy and congregants have parallel experiences of soul-deep renewal."

— Tim Shapiro, Indianapolis Center for Congregations

"Speaking from a place of deep appreciation for the sacred art of ministry combined with respect for the mental, spiritual, and physical labor of pastors, Rob gifts us with wisdom for how to honor and strengthen the church. This book reminds us that to rest is to trust God. Revitalized pastors return from sabbatical energized to live out their dreams. This is good news for the church! Thankfully, Rob's book is here to show us the way."

— Sarah Lund, United Church of Christ's Minister for Disabilities and Mental Health Justice

"Here's a trusted voice for congregations and ministers who are planning a pastoral sabbatical. Saler's style and insight honor the sacred, Spirit-led relationship between pastors and congregations. His helpfully defined terms, diverse examples, and practical wisdom address with care and hope the common questions and concerns associated with a renewal leave."

— William B. Kincaid, Christian Theological Seminary, Indianapolis

"Rob Saler has given us an ode to joy for the renewal of congregations and clergy. This is a practical guide to a courageous life-giving experience. Clergy renewal leaves can be the whole church's version of Bach's "Gloria.""

— Michael Mather, pastor, author of *Having Nothing, Possessing Everything: Finding Abundant Communities in Unexpected Places*

PLANNING SABBATICALS

A GUIDE FOR CONGREGATIONS AND THEIR PASTORS

ROBERT C. SALER

chalice press

Saint Louis, Missouri

An imprint of Christian Board of Publication

Copyright ©2019 by Robert Saler.

All rights reserved. For permission to reuse content, please contact Copyright Clearance Center, 222 Rosewood Drive, Danvers, MA 01923, (978) 750-8400, www.copyright.com.

ChalicePress.com

Print ISBN: 9780827231795
EPUB: 9780827231801
EPDF: 9780827231818

Printed in the United States of America

Contents

Acknowledgments

I wish to gratefully acknowledge the opportunity to engage with congregations and pastors across the United States that has come with the privilege of serving as director of the Lilly Endowment Clergy Renewal Programs at Christian Theological Seminary. This work has brought me into close proximity with some of the best minds thinking about congregational dynamics and the renewal of ministry today. While too many have shared wisdom to for me to hope to count them all, conversations with Bill Kincaid, Tim Shapiro, Christopher Coble, Craig Dykstra, Brian Williams, Chanon Ross, John Wimmer, Jessicah Duckworth, Verity Jones, Jean Smith, Marty Wright, Mike Mather, Philip James, Phil Goff, Elise Erikson Barrett, David Odom, Marty Wright, Leah Gunning Francis, Claude Alexander, Frank Thomas, and Patricia Bouteneff have been particularly memorable. Callie Smith, who has served with distinction as my colleague and associate director of the Clergy Renewal Programs, deserves special mention as one whose insight has proven invaluable in strengthening the cause of clergy sabbaticals for thousands of congregations. I am grateful to my academic home, Christian Theological Seminary in Indianapolis, for the willingness of faculty and staff to host these programs and to welcome so many pastors and congregations into its orbit of concern.

I'm grateful to Chalice Press and its entire excellent editorial team for providing such support and care in bringing this project into fruition. The press exudes energy on behalf of the 21st -century church in all its challenge and promise, and that has made it an ideal home for this book.

To the congregations and pastors who step out in faith to pursue the chance to strengthen their shared ministry together by means of a renewal leave for their pastor, I honor you and hope the words shared in this book stand as tribute to your fidelity and courage.

Introduction

A congregation on the north side of a large city was in a situation shared by so many other congregations: the demographics of the neighborhood around it were changing rapidly, and the members found themselves wondering how they could improve their ability to be hospitable to their new neighbors (many of whom were recent immigrants finding their way in the United States for the first time). So the congregation and its pastor had an idea: the pastor would take a sabbatical to venture abroad, to Nigeria, where the pastor had always wanted to go but also would know very few people. In other words, the pastor would need to be hosted. She would need to rely on the hospitality of others to find her way. The experience of being dislocated, of needing to be hosted, would give her a small taste of what the church's neighbors were experiencing, and this existential insight would provide her with a new frame with which to think about leading the congregation through its process of welcome.

Equally importantly, though, while the pastor was away, the congregation was not idle! During the pastor's three-month sabbatical, the congregation would call on several biblical scholars and theologians to visit the congregation and teach it about the crucial place of hospitality in the Christian life—hospitality in its biblical, historical, and theological dimensions. Whether it was Abraham hosting angels in the book of Genesis or Jesus sending his disciples out to receive (or not) welcome from villages on the road, the stories of the Bible enlivened the congregation's imagination while their pastor was away.

And then, when the reunion between the pastor and the congregation happened, a kind of alchemy occurred. The pastor had been touched at a soul level by the experience of being out

1

of her element, but even more so by the continual kindness she encountered during her travel challenges. She had stories to tell, but also, more importantly, a deeply personal vigor for creating a space of hospitality for all who were dislocated in her own congregational context. Meanwhile, with the minds and hearts of so many members on those scriptural stories of hosting and being hosted, the congregation collectively had new ears to hear the pastor's testimony. Its members also had a fierce new energy for asking complex questions about how they could best be hosts in their community—not simply inviting their new neighbors to worship, but to accompany them in multifaceted ways as they sought to make their homes in an unfamiliar place. The renewal period, comprised of the pastor's sabbatical and the congregation's intentional use of the time, provided both a spiritual foundation and a holy goad toward a new season of shared ministry together.

This story is a particularly dramatic instance of the kind of alchemy that I want to explore in this book—the kind of magic that happens when a pastor's period of temporarily stepping away from the day-to-day responsibilities of ministry *and* the congregation's intentionality in using that time for its own spiritual growth weave together in such a way that the shared ministry between the pastor and congregation are renewed and strengthened.

Maybe "magic" is not the right word, since "magic" implies a kind of technique, a sort of "do this and this result will happen" mentality. Christians prefer to speak, not of magic, but of the work of the Holy Spirit—the wind that blows where it will (Jn. 3:8), but brings unpredictable blessings and abundant surprise wherever it does its work. The Greek word for spirit, *pneuma,* leads Christian theologians to describe certain things as "pneumatological"—the work of the Holy Spirit. I believe that a successful renewal leave experience is, in fact, "pneumatological" in precisely that sense—when it goes well, we Christians bring our best efforts and intentionality and are once again surprised by what God's Spirit can do. The blessings go above and beyond our expectations. The Holy Spirit creates new energy.

Not every renewal leave experience will be like the one described above. Sometimes the ambitions and the results of the experience are simpler: a pastor loves C.S. Lewis and travels to England and Ireland in order to walk in Lewis's footsteps while the congregation back home reads *The Screwtape Letters* together, and the result is that the congregation is able to appreciate more deeply the regular Lewis quotes that the pastor puts in a sermon. The pastor spends time in the Holy Land seeing biblical sights, and the congregation notices a new level of dramatic vision and detail in the pastor's Bible studies.

But simpler is not less holy. The same Spirit-led alchemy is at play any time a congregation honors its pastor and the ministry it shares with its pastor by pursuing a renewal experience. And, just as in Jesus' parables, sometimes it is the simplest and humblest of seeds planted that eventually bear the richest fruit in ministry.

What Do We Mean by "Renewal Experience"?

It would be good to get some terms clear that I will be using throughout the book.

As the title of the book promises, I intend for this book to be a guide for congregations that are exploring the possibility of sending their pastors on sabbatical. For the purposes of this book, I will define "pastoral sabbatical" as any extended period (I'll be recommending three-to-four months) in which the pastor steps away from the day-to-day practices of ministry in order to focus on their spiritual development with an eye toward returning to the congregation with renewed energy for ministry.

Obviously, and as we will discuss at length, such focus can take any number of forms and center on lots of different activities; there is no one set model for what a sabbatical should look like, and when you consider the fact that God has given each of us—pastors included—different sorts of passions and gifts and life circumstances, then the variety of sabbaticals should be as wide as the blessed variety of pastors taking them. *But a "pastoral sabbatical" is, at minimum, an extended period of time in which the pastor is away from the congregation pursuing a variety of intentionally renewing activities.*

What are those activities? Possibilities are virtually endless—as are the stories of what pastors have done with this time! A pastoral sabbatical can be travel abroad, to experience new cultures and have the imagination fired. It can be intensive time spent with loved ones, forging deep bonds that can continue to endure and thrive within the demands of ministry often placed upon the pastor's whole family. It can be deep study, of theology or the Bible or history or the lives of inspiring figures. It can be time spent in creating—art, photography, painting, writing. It can be a time spent regaining health—exercising more, sleeping more deeply, eating better. It can be a time of recommitting to spiritual practices, such as prayer or daily devotions. It can be pilgrimage. It can be ease. Indeed, the best sabbaticals will encompass multiple activities, all with the goal of each individual pastor finding the rhythm that speaks to the soul.

Some pastors take courses in new subjects. Some pastors seclude themselves in cabins and write poems. Some pastors travel the world and see sights that are spiritually meaningful to them. Some reconnect with mentors from the past; some meet spiritual heroes in the present. Many reconnect with family and loved ones in unstructured time. Some sabbaticals are spent on motorcycles, some on hiking trails, some on airplanes, some on beaches, some in monasteries. Indeed, most sabbaticals that I know of combine a whole host of these activities into a unified whole that speaks to various aspects of the pastor's soul (more on this below).

That said, this book is about more than sabbaticals. There is (thankfully) a growing number of books out there that give advice to pastors specifically about how to plan their own sabbaticals. But what I have in mind in this book is addressing the total package: not just the pastor's sabbatical (as important as that is), but the congregation's part as well. In other words, a "renewal experience" *includes* the pastoral sabbatical, but is *more* than that.

When I say "renewal period" or "renewal experience," I mean the *shared* experience between the pastor and the congregation. In my view, pastoral sabbaticals are *one* (important) piece of the broader picture. If you are a member of a congregation or a pastor of a congregation reading this book, I want you to think of the entire renewal experience—the early dreaming stages, the logistical planning, the pastor's leave, the congregation's activities, the reunion, and the shared ministry together after— as part of one unified process.

The term "sabbatical," even though it has deep biblical roots in the concept of "Sabbath rest," also carries overtones of academia. Academic sabbaticals are product-oriented: a professor takes a sabbatical to go away and write a book, or research a new skill. One can imagine a kind of pastoral sabbatical in which the pastor is going away to focus on skill-building—say, continuing education or sermon preparation or some such thing. But this is not what I have in mind when I say "renewal leave" or "sabbatical" in this book. In this book, the purpose of a pastoral sabbatical is not to produce a certain product, but for the pastor to regain energy and focus and connection to inner spiritual resources—all for the sake of being renewed for a long ministry with their congregation. The notion of "renewal" for shared ministry together keeps the focus where it needs to be—not on the individual pastor solely, but on the entire congregation that undertakes the adventure of the renewal period.

I was a pastor of a congregation for a time, which goes part of the way in explaining why in this book I am so adamant that something so significant as a pastoral sabbatical be undertaken as a shared endeavor between the pastor and the congregation. But the main fuel for that belief has been my work over the last six years as director of the Lilly Endowment Clergy Renewal Programs, which gives grants to over 150 congregations a year to support their pastors taking renewal leaves.[1] In that work, I have interfaced with thousands of congregations at various stages of discernment and planning for a renewal leave experience. And there is one lesson more than any other that has surfaced time and time again: the most successful pastoral sabbatical programs involve the entire congregation from start to finish.

As we will see, there are logistical reasons for involving the congregation in the sabbatical program: heavy congregational involvement at every stage of discerning, planning, and undertaking a renewal leave experience helps to ward off a lot of potential difficulties. But the positive rationale is even more compelling! If, as I believe, the point of a successful pastoral renewal leave is to strengthen the shared ministry of a pastor and congregation so that they can pursue their calling together with even more passion, then deep engagement between the pastor and the congregation at every step is a positive gift that will yield major dividends throughout the process.

---

[1] In saying this about my work, I want to be clear that the anecdotes that are peppered throughout this book, unless otherwise noted, come from a broad range of discussions about pastoral sabbaticals and congregations' experience (not simply those participating in the Lilly Endowment Clergy Renewal Programs specifically); moreover, I have left any identifying details sufficiently vague as to protect the relevant confidentiality of pastors and their congregations.

In saying this, I certainly don't want to give the impression that only parish pastors deserve sabbaticals or can benefit from them. As I'll try to make clear in the first chapter, I think that all sorts of professionals—from nurses to elementary school teachers to business executives and beyond—can (and ideally *should*) benefit from sabbaticals.

Moreover, I don't want to disregard the fact that a great deal of vital Christian ministry and leadership takes place in venues other than congregational ministry. Hospital chaplains, judicatory officials such as bishops and their assistants, intentional interim pastors, college ministry leaders, and others do incredible work on behalf of the church and the world. If someone in that sort of ministry setting is contemplating or actively planning a sabbatical, my hope is that at least some of what I say in this book will be applicable. That said, my framework in this book will be congregations seeking to undertake this renewal leave work alongside their pastors. Congregations are wonderful, complicated, unique places, and so we will focus attention there.

My hope for this book is that it is the sort of thing that congregational leaders (elders, council members, vestry, parish mutual ministry teams, or whatever leadership your congregation has in place) can read and discuss, together with their pastors, at any stage of the renewal leave process. Some congregations have long histories of pastors taking sabbaticals. Others might be hearing about the possibility for the first time. Some congregations will be made up of members[2] who are immediately supportive of pursuing the

---

[2]Throughout the book I'll use the term *members* even though I know that many congregations now either do not have formal "membership" at all, or else membership is limited to a smaller section of a larger body of worshipers and active participants in the life of the congregation. So *members* should be understood as shorthand for everyone in the congregation who is active in its life and has a stake in its mission going well.

idea; other congregations may need months or even years to properly discern how best to shape a renewal period for their own contexts. Again, variety is of the Spirit and it is beautiful.

But wherever a congregation finds itself, I offer this little book as a "thinking-with" companion that stimulates excellent conversations among pastors and their people. I would like for this to be helpful for elder boards, church councils, vestries, or whatever partners in ministry help to guide major decisions in congregations—because renewal leaves are major decisions! There are lots of excellent resources available aimed at pastors who are planning their sabbaticals, and I will try to point to most of those in the pages ahead.

In my work, we often hear congregations attest that the process of dreaming and planning together was the most helpful part of the whole experience, and so this book is meant to be an aid to help that process be as rich as it can be. While there is some "practical" advice spread throughout the book, it is mostly designed as an invitation to dream well and wisely, and to let the wisdom of others inform what will ultimately be a highly personal process for the congregation and the pastor.

One more thing should be said at the outset, and it's something that we all know but still bears repeating: courage and honor are related. It takes courage for congregations to bless their pastors being away for an extended period, just as it takes courage for pastors to unplug from their beloved ministry settings. It especially takes courage on all sides to explore this possibility if the congregation has never had a history of pastors taking sabbaticals. If you are reading this book, if you are curious about beginning the process of discerning whether and how God might be calling you to consider this renewal leave possibility for your congregation, then I commend you on your courage *and* your willingness to honor your pastor and your pastor's loved ones by this action.

To honor ministry is to strengthen it. To embrace rest is to demonstrate confidence in the energy that God can pour into revitalized pastors and congregations. This book will be an invitation to dream about what that might look like for your pastor and your congregation.

1

Shared Journey

Why Pastoral Renewal Leaves Are Good for Congregations

This book will contain several mantras, and this chapter introduces one of the most important ones: *the better the renewal time for the congregation, the better the sabbatical time for the pastor, and vice versa.* If the congregation has a good experience with the renewal leave, it will not only help sustain the benefits of the pastor's sabbatical across the next years of shared ministry, but it will help ease both the mind of the pastor *and* the minds of the congregation members *during* the leave period.

So with that in mind, let's explore the dual benefit of clergy renewal leaves: a refreshed pastor and an inspired congregation.

A Refreshed and Reenergized Pastor

As we mentioned before, pastoral sabbaticals are not product-driven. We can put that a different way: the main "product," so to speak, of a successful pastoral sabbatical is a refreshed and renewed pastor.

At the outset, we should stipulate two things: a pastor's work is not necessarily harder than that of other congregational members; but *it is hard in a different way.* In other words, the challenges of pastoral ministry in congregations, while not necessarily *more* intense than, say, an emergency medical technician or a public-school teacher or a construction worker, are *uniquely* intense in ways that pastoral renewal leaves can address.

Pastors serve many roles. Depending on the size and nature of the church, they are counselors, weekly public speakers, worship planners, physical plant consultants, Bible and theology teachers, youth faith encouragers, broken toilet fixers, community leaders, social justice advocates, and fundraisers. In communities where English is rare, they are often tutors, immigration counselors, and cultural mentors. They conduct weddings and funerals. Often, they are "on call" for congregational emergencies 24/7, and these emergencies might arise at 2 a.m.—or, smack in the middle of a planned family vacation. They work on Sundays and holidays. It is, as Marva Dawn says, an "odd and wondrous" calling, but it is also an intense one.

And that is just the visible, external work. At an even deeper level, much of the work of the pastor is internal and invisible. Put simply, pastors care at very deep levels, about a great many people, at the most intense points of those peoples' lives—when loved ones die, when tragedies befall children, when a routine day becomes a scary hospital stay, when God seems far away. Even accompanying their people in times of joy—weddings, graduations, periods of feeling intensely held by God—can produce what psychologists call "eustress": vital, excited states of heightened emotion that feel wonderful but can also sometimes prove to be overwhelming. (Think of a time when you may have found yourself weeping during or after a joyous occasion; you know you "should" be happy, but your body still feels flooded by emotions in a way that drains you.) In other words, much of the work of being a pastor is internal, emotional, and intense in ways that draw upon deep reserves of emotional and spiritual resources.

Fortunately, most pastors have deep wells. Pastors are trained—often in seminaries, but often too by mentorship and hands-on learning—to sustain themselves in prayer, study of God's word, intellectual pursuits, and delight in family and friends. Healthy pastors are trained to engage in all the tasks mentioned above (and countless others) from a position of deep centeredness.

Craig Dykstra, an expert in the dynamics of pastoral ministry, writes the following:

> Every day pastors are immersed in a constant, and sometimes nearly chaotic, interplay of meaning-filled relationships and demands. They attend to scripture; struggle to discern the gospel's call and demand on them and their congregations in particular contexts; lead worship, preach and teach; respond to requests for help of all kinds from myriad people in need; live with children, youth and adults through life cycles marked by both great joy and profound sadness; and take responsibility for the unending work of running an organization with buildings, budgets, and public relations and personnel issues.

> In the midst of the interplay of all this and more, pastors become who they are; indeed, pastors are transformed. The unique confluence of all these forces both requires and gives shape to an imagination marked by characteristics and features unlike those required in any other walk of life. Life lived long enough and fully enough in the pastoral office gives rise to a way of seeing in depth and of creating new realities that is an

indispensable gift to the church, to all who are members of it, and indeed to public life and to the world.[1]

To be healthy, to achieve the "seeing in depth" and "creating new realities" that Dykstra describes, pastors need powerful internal spiritual resources as they move creatively and imaginatively throughout the work of ministry.

If you'll forgive a pun, though, the logic of clergy sabbaticals is that such resources are indeed "renew-able." Prayer, spiritual disciplines, delight in loved ones and hobbies, and rest all require time and attention to cultivate—as we will see throughout this book.

Another of the mantras that I will repeat throughout the book, and that I will introduce now, is as follows: *sabbaticals are for healthy pastors in healthy congregations.* We'll spend a lot of time in later chapters exploring more about what that means, but here I bring it up as a way of emphasizing that sabbatical leaves are about revitalizing and renewing healthy pastors who could use some time to re-center in the very things that allow them to be excellent at their work: prayer, God's word, spiritual practices, and delight in their loved ones. Soul care requires soul maintenance.

Laurie Haller, a Methodist pastor who wrote a memoir about her sabbatical experience, had this to say about the effects of the months away spent in exploration and prayer:

> I feel more centered and calm than I have in 25 years. Most people will not observe that simply by looking at me. I am the same on the outside. Inside, however, I have been changed and transformed. It's not to say

---

[1]Craig Dykstra, "Imagination and the Pastoral Life," available at https://www.religion-online.org/article/imagination-and-the-pastoral-life/.

I won't be busy come next Monday. Being a pastor in a large church will always be demanding. And I don't think God necessarily wants me to be less busy. God only wants me to realign my priorities. God wants to be the center of my attention. When love of God comes before anything else, I am convinced that I will be able to stay centered and grounded.[2]

Congregations whose pastors have returned from sabbaticals often report that their pastors exhibit, simultaneously, a renewed energy but also a deeper calm. This great combination of energy and centeredness can positively impact everything from sermons to Bible studies to committee leadership to pastoral care. It is a lesson at the heart of our Christian faith: when we are centered in God, the labor that we are called to do in God's vineyard moves with greater ease, but also more excellence.

There is a line in the movie *Top Gun* in which the commander says to the new pilots, "Gentlemen, you are the top 1 percent of all naval aviators. The elite. The best of the best. We'll make you better." Renewal leaves are not for fixing broken or burnt-out pastors, or for healing deeply wounded congregations. They are for excellent pastors who want to re-center in order to continue to be excellent.

I once sat next to a pastor at a conference dinner while they discussed their sabbatical leave. They said something that has stayed with me, and that I have come to value as a powerful image for what sabbaticals can do. "I thought I would come back full," they said. "Full of new ideas for church programs, full of insights for sermons, full of outreach strategies. Instead, I came back empty. Emptied of pride, emptied of ego, emptied

---

[2]Laurie Haller, *Recess: Rediscovering Play and Purpose* (Canton: Cass Community Publishing, 2015), 218.

of thinking that it was all about me. It turns out that I didn't need for God to fill me; I needed time for God to empty me. And when I came back to my congregation empty, that's when God was ready to fill all of us with new possibilities that I would have been too full to see if God had not emptied me first."

We'll say a lot more about what this means in future chapters, but for now we can name the fact that one of the two main goals of any successful renewal program is a revitalized and refreshed pastor. What is the other main goal?

An Inspired Congregation

I'll say it over and over again in this book: what happens with the pastor and the pastor's loved ones during a renewal period is only half the equation. Renewal leaves are not just about the pastor. A successful pastoral renewal leave is just as much about what happens before, during, and after the leave on the part of the congregation. The renewal leave does not "belong" to the pastor; the whole process, start to finish, belongs to the congregation. This is the recipe for success during *and* after the renewal period.

What can happen on the congregation's end? My favorite story of this comes from my colleague Marty, who pastors a dynamic congregation in central Indiana. Marty has taken two clergy sabbaticals during his tenure in the congregation, and the two yielded quite different—but ultimately equally powerful— experiences for the congregation.

During Marty's first leave, his congregation was nervous but excited to undertake the adventure of stepping up in his absence. While a variety of guest preachers filled the pulpit to preach, it was key congregational leaders who volunteered to take on more tasks in the day-to-day administration of the church that really sparked a new season of energy in the church while Marty was away. When he returned, he joked that he had to put his ego in check when he saw that attendance and giving had actually gone up in his absence!

(*Note*: the congregation's deeply sincere, warm welcome upon his return helped to ease his mind on the "feeling wanted" front!)

But the congregation's lay leadership stepping up during this first leave had another effect. Once some members took a turn at supervising some ministries that had been on the pastor's plate, they found that they didn't want to give them up! Sunday school superintending, music ministries, youth group supervision—things that, in that congregation, had traditionally all been on the pastor's plate—were suddenly disbursed permanently throughout the lay leadership. Given that one of Marty's insights on his sabbatical was that he was probably taking on too many tasks as pastor within the congregation and thus needed to trust his people to exercise more leadership, the timing was perfect. Not only did existing leaders feel empowered to take on more responsibility, but new leaders had come out of the woodwork, ready to help the entire congregation shoulder the tasks of a newly energized season of ministry.

When Marty left for his second sabbatical, seven years later, the congregation might have expected that the same thing would happen: greater attendance, a surge of energy among the members. But when Marty returned after four months away, his senior leaders reported a concern: attendance had gone down during this second leave, and, moreover, a number of major congregational leaders had seemingly disappeared over the summer. What had changed? The leaders were not sure.

Undaunted, Marty took to the pulpit on the Sunday after he returned, and...attendance and giving surged back. Upon reflection, Marty and his staff realized that, during this second leave, congregational leaders themselves had decided to take a sabbatical! Rather than digging in and taking on more heavy lifting as they had during the first renewal leave, many congregational leaders had followed their pastor's lead and had spent the summer focusing quietly on their own spiritual health, their own families, their own sense of centeredness. And, like Marty, when they returned, they returned rejuvenated and ready to grow even further!

At this point, it will not surprise you to learn that Marty and his congregation had worked very closely together in the discernment and design of the two renewal periods. In order to achieve the Spirit-filled alchemy, the process had to be collaborate from the very earliest stages all the way to the end of the leave. We'll see more about what this can look like in chapters to come.

But for now, what we can know for sure is that the flip side of a renewed pastor is a rejuvenated congregation. These are the two main goals of clergy renewal leaves, and they go hand in hand. This is not the congregation giving the pastor a sabbatical as a kind of favor. This is the congregation and the pastor, *together,* embarking on the renewal experience. It may seem like a small difference, but it makes all the difference!

And the two goals mutually reinforce each other. The better the renewal period goes for the congregation, the more fulfilling the sabbatical will be for the pastor, and vice versa. In a healthy congregational renewal process, what's good for the pastor is not somehow in competition with the needs of the congregation; instead, the two build on each other in surprising and Spirit-filled ways.

Congregations who complete renewal leaves successfully are built up by the experience in a number of ways. They gain new insights into the ways their ministry is about more than what the pastor does, and they gain confidence that their staff and members can take on leadership in the pastor's absence in ways that might well continue even after the pastor has returned. The pastor's sabbatical gives the congregation permission to explore similar topics and themes as the pastor who is away, "journeying alongside" their pastor so that wisdom and insights can be shared upon the pastor's return. And the ability for congregations to honor beloved pastors (and families!) with the gift of renewal can produce a significant morale boost for congregations of all kinds.

As Melissa Bane Sevier remarks, "Pastoral leaders who are healthy find they stay longer in their congregations, and congregations with healthy pastors are healthy themselves. Our culture may idolize the workaholic leader, but that leadership style does not best serve the congregation. Balanced leaders make for balanced congregations."[3]

———————

Congregations have different levels of ambition for what they want out of renewal periods. For some congregations, the chance to honor the pastor and have them come back refreshed is enough—and that is okay! For other congregations, the leave presents a chance for deep dives into areas of passion for the congregation—study, service, introspection, etc. That is just fine as well.

The main thing to do is to always have the courage to make it about *your* congregation and *your* context. What would renewal look like for you, in all of your blessed God-given particularity?

---

[3]Melissa Bane Sevier, *Journeying Toward Renewal: A Spiritual Companion for Pastoral Sabbaticals* (Bethesda, Md.: Alban Institute, 2002), 63.

What is special about your congregation and your pastor that can lead you to work together to craft an experience that no other congregation would delight in as much?

If you are dreaming along these lines, and if you are starting to envision what this might look like for your congregation, then the next question will be: How do you get started having the conversation? This is what we will turn to next.

2

Beginning the Dialogue

Some Common Concerns

How to begin the conversation?

Pastors and congregation members hear about the possibility of renewal leaves from a variety of sources these days: denominational gatherings, websites, and (especially) other congregations. If you are holding this book, chances are that this possibility has come onto your congregation's radar and you are eager to get started with the discussion (or at least intrigued enough to keep the dialogue about the possibility open!)

But once the congregation is ready to explore the idea of the pastor taking a sabbatical, there may be some initial concern. This is especially true if the congregation or the pastor has had no prior experience with sabbaticals. So it is good to assume that the congregation will need some time to process the idea, and plenty of space to dialogue about whether it is the right time in the life of the congregation to pursue this opportunity.

In the first section of this chapter, I'll list some common objections to renewal leaves that are heard from congregation members (as well as some ideas on how to respond); in the second section, we'll address reasons why pastors are sometimes reluctant to take these leaves.

The main thing to note before getting into these concerns is that the best posture for those who are in favor of the congregation undertaking discernment about a renewal leave is not one of defensiveness; you are not trying to "win" the argument, since overcoming opposition without eventually getting those with questions excited about the possibilities for the leave will be counterproductive. You don't want to win an argument; you want to build consensus. As Richard Bullock and Richard J. Bruesehoff note, "What must finally undergird renewal leave is the unreserved commitment of all members of the staff and of the elected boards [or, we may say, visible congregational leaders in any role]. This does not mean that everyone is equally enthusiastic about sabbatical leave, but it does mean that everyone can and will publicly support the renewal leave without reservation."[1]

I can't emphasize this enough: time spent engaging in thoughtful dialogue around this topic with key stakeholders within the congregation, or really anyone who has a say in how the congregation makes important decisions, will pay dividends in every subsequent stage of the process. The discernment dialogue should not be rushed. Whether it takes three weeks or three years, it is time well spent.

Congregations, depending on size and denomination (or lack of denomination), will have different ways of formally starting the conversation. A church of 40 members might call an ad hoc meeting; a church of four thousand members might start with a formal proposal at a governing board. Treat the decision

---

[1]Richard Bullock and Richard J. Bruesehoff, *Clergy Renewal: The Alban Guide to Sabbatical Planning* (Herndon, Va.: Alban Institute, 2000), 45.

as you would any other significant decision in the life of the congregation. I suggest that you introduce it using the same procedures that you would use to float the idea of starting a capital campaign or a building project—that may seem extreme, but it is a good example of the scale of buy-in that it is helpful to have for renewal periods! The more seriously it is treated in its introduction to various congregational stakeholders, the more they might catch a vision of how beneficial it all is.

A Note of Caution: Tired or Burnt Out?

One further note—this one from our experience with the Lilly Endowment Clergy Renewal Programs. It is rare that the renewal leaves that we fund go badly, but when they do it is almost always because of one of two factors. Either the congregation was not as on board with the renewal experience (especially the pastor being gone) as the pastor thought, or the pastor was "burnt out" enough to be in need of a more serious intervention than just a sabbatical.

One note on that: One often hears that clergy sabbaticals are a way to address "burnout." To be sure, it is true that sabbaticals—when taken within the context of a broader strategy of self-care, spiritual practices, and other modes of maintaining vitality in ministry—can be a component in *preventing* burnout. But—and I want to stress this very clearly—pastoral renewal leaves are *not* an effective instrument for addressing burnout once it has set in. Renewal leaves are for healthy pastors in healthy congregations; to use them as a kind of desperation healing technique is to risk exacerbating rather than fixing any problems. Burnt-out pastors need interventions such as counseling, mentorship, consultation with trusted guides, and (in some cases) perhaps even a season away from congregational leadership; what they do not need is time away that will likely serve to mask rather than address the deeper symptoms of unhealth.

Now, to be clear, "tired" is not the same as "unhealthy." It is possible (and indeed common) for excellent pastors to reach a season in ministry in which they are tired enough to benefit from a chance to break from the day-to-day demands of ministry; these pastors are excellent candidates to benefit from a renewal program. But there are modes of exhaustion that come much closer to full-on burnout, and in those cases sabbaticals can easily do more harm than good.

If you are a pastor contemplating sabbatical, then take an honest self-inventory. Are you still excited about ministry, but can see the benefit of some time away? Or, do you have to drag yourself into the office every morning? Are you tired, or *exhausted*? Do you get excited at the thought of renewing yourself for more ministry where you are, or do you feel like deeper work needs to be done in order to heal your mind, body, and soul? If you are tired but happy, then sabbatical might be right for you; if you are exhausted and on the edge, then seek other kinds of counseling and intervention before your congregation pursues a sabbatical program for you.

The following recommended answers to common questions all assume that no renewal program will be undertaken without the congregation being brought fully on board, and that the congregation considering doing this is doing so for a pastor in a state of health and enthusiasm for ministry (since these are, in my opinion, the *only* circumstances under which a renewal leave should be taken).

Common Congregational Concerns

1. I Work Hard Too! Why Don't I Get a Sabbatical?

It can be hard for congregation members who themselves work long hours at jobs to understand why the pastor should be singled out for the opportunity to take a sabbatical. This is completely understandable. There are two strategies for hearing and addressing this concern well.

The first is to acknowledge that, in an ideal world, every worker *should* get a sabbatical to get re-centered in the things that make a vocation worthwhile (whether that vocation happens to be the job itself or some other aspect of life—for many people, what they do to earn money is not necessarily their vocation!). In his book *Power Sabbatical: The Break that Makes a Difference*, Robert Levine outlines the ways that sabbaticals can reenergize and refocus workers in a whole variety of contexts: business, medicine, labor, etc.[2] Corporate sabbatical programs are becoming more and more common. Congregations that are excited about the prospect of renewal leaves for their pastors might try to encourage their people to seek out similar opportunities in their own work; perhaps congregations can even serve as advocates or resource pools in trying to create those opportunities.

But that said, as mentioned above, there is a kind of spiritual intensity *and* 24-hour demand cycle that is, if not fully unique to pastoral ministry, at least always present within it. Pastors have to be spiritually "on" over long periods of time, and their church responsibilities often mean that they (and, by extension, their families) are working when others are resting. The emotional, spiritual, and physical intensity of pastoral ministry warrants specialized attention—not because it's "harder," but because its challenges are unique. A unified renewal experience between the pastor and the congregation is a proven way to address those needs.

---

[2]See Robert Levine, *Power Sabbatical: The Break that Makes a Difference* (Findhorn Press, 2007).

So when in dialogue with congregation members who are indignant at the thought that the pastor is receiving "special treatment," it is helpful to do a number of things.

First, it may be good to stress that it is not a matter of the pastor "deserving" a sabbatical more than others in the church; every hard worker deserves to have time to renew and refresh, and congregations should play a role in advocating for that to happen in whatever way works for a given job. Here, as in other areas, it may be on the church to help model a different way of being for society at large, and the church should not miss that opportunity.[3] The drive for all of us to work until we collapse is part of a social idolatry of achievement, and sabbaticals can be combined with a larger encouragement for Sabbath-keeping across the entire congregation as a way of challenging this idol within our culture. Every Christian tradition, in its own way, stresses that our ultimate worth comes from God's grace and not our own achievements in this life, and the church advocating for sabbatical practices for *all* might be a powerful part of its ministry in the future.

Having said that, this conversation is also an excellent time for congregation members to reflect upon what it is that they think their pastor does. Think about it: this conversation about the pastor's many roles and responsibilities might be the first time in a long time for many congregations when they have taken stock of the scope of the pastor's job. You hear talk of "pastor appreciation days"; well, this conversation can be an extended pastoral appreciation unto itself! "I had no idea how much the pastor actually does until we sat down and began talking about it" is a common refrain among congregations that begin this process. Coming to deeper realization of how

---

[3]Cf. Walter Brueggemann, *Sabbath as Resistance: Saying No to the Culture of Now* (Louisville: Westminster John Knox Press, 2014) for more on this theme of the church's insistence upon rest and renewal as countercultural.

intense the pastoral calling can be is already deeply beneficial relationship-building between the pastor and congregation.

Third, and this is crucial: it is important here, as always, to gently remind everyone that the pastor's sabbatical is just one component of the congregation's larger renewal leave. Language here is crucial: the congregation is not "giving" the pastor a sabbatical or "letting" the pastor go on sabbatical. Instead, the congregation, as a whole, in partnership with its pastor, is undertaking a renewal period that is for the benefit for the entire congregation. This is shared work, in hopes of shared benefits.

2. Is This Just a Vacation?

It may be that the pastor's sabbatical has some activities in it that look a lot like things one might do on a vacation. Maybe it is a dream for the pastor's family to go on a Disney cruise or a trip to the Grand Canyon. Maybe a group of seminary friends wants to catch up over a baseball game. Maybe a theater-loving pastor wants to get inspiration from Broadway shows. Sabbatical itineraries are as unique as the pastors and congregations that plan them, and a key part of renewal is fun—often, fun times with family and loved ones. One pastor I know took his son on a motorcycle tour of the national parks of the Midwest, speaking to him about hopes and dreams for college and beyond at every stop. Memories that last a lifetime are often made. So what makes this sabbatical and not vacation?

The difference between vacation and sabbatical has less to do with activities and more to do with intent. What are the activities for? What is the purpose? A vacation is intended for pure relaxation and refreshment. A sabbatical, on the contrary, should be designed with this question in mind: "What activities will renew the pastor's heart and ministry for long-term ministry in the congregation?" A vacation is recreation; a sabbatical is focused renewal.

We will talk more in future chapters about some activities that can go into a pastor's renewal leave. But for now, the question is less, "What?" and more, "Why?" *Why* is a particular activity the right one for this pastor and these people to pursue? Why will these activities get at the goals stated above: a reenergized pastor and a revitalized congregation?

When people wonder aloud if a sabbatical is just a fancy word for vacation, it provides another chance to point out that renewal is for the whole congregation—that the pastor's sabbatical is just one component of the broader whole. But it is also a reminder to commit, nondefensively, to the process of finding activities for both the pastor and the congregation that get at the stated goals of the renewal period. Is the pastor's goal to create quality bonds with their children apart from the day-to-day demands of ministry? Then certain child-friendly activities might get at that goal the best, and the congregation can follow suit. Is the pastor's goal to have an embodied experience of the Holy Land so as to enhance his sense of the spaces discussed in scripture? Then, that implies a different strategy.

If the goals for the renewal program are stated clearly, *early* and *often* in the process, then it will be easier to identify activities that are not too "vacation-y" but are, rather, focused on deep renewal for the pastor and congregation.

Another point that should be mentioned is that, as a rule, sabbaticals are longer than vacations. In the programs that I direct, we have found that three-to-four months of unbroken time away is ideal. It takes a while for pastors to get into a rhythm in which they are not thinking of their congregations first thing in the morning, and it also takes time for pastors to reenter slowly so as to avoid immediately falling back into pre-sabbatical patterns. While pertinent activities and good planning are essential ingredients of a renewal leave, the core ingredient is simple and irreplaceable: time. The very gift of time to live into patterns of rest and refocus is often, more so than any particular activity, the thing that produces the most potent transformation in pastors who take sabbaticals.

3. Will the Church Survive without the Pastor?

Many people fear that their congregations will falter without their pastors; indeed, this fear is often a compliment! When congregations love and trust their pastors, of course it is natural for them to fear what might happen when the pastor is away. Will attendance drop? Or giving? Who will handle all the tasks, known and unknown, that pastors need to tackle during the week? While most renewal leaves involve guest pastors coming in to preach, preside at sacraments, and cover some pastoral care duties, renewal leaves are also excellent times for the congregation to find out what its people can do.

Remember the story of Marty and his congregation from earlier? He came back to discover that lay leaders had stepped into roles that they did not want to "give back" after he returned, and both his ministry and the congregation's was strengthened as a result. Time after time, when we hear from congregations about how things went while their pastor was on sabbatical, we hear stories of congregation members stepping up and taking on tasks that had previously been the purview of the pastor.

Renewal periods can give congregations courage: courage to realize that their members have gifts—some of which are known, some of which are unknown. Congregations that undergo this experience often find that previously quiet members "come out of the woodwork" to take on new tasks. The importance of this should not be underestimated! It is often said that, in many congregations, "20 percent of the people do

90 percent of the work." One of the most concrete, tangible outcomes of renewal periods for congregations is the chance for members to discover leadership and service gifts that they might not have known they have.

Meanwhile, to borrow a point from the psychology of relationships: interpersonal relationships function best when a person who has integrity and wholeness as an individual chooses to enter into relationship with a similarly healthy person. In the same way, it is better for pastors and for congregations if congregations love their pastor but are not dependent upon the pastor to keep the congregation's life together intact. In my office, when we receive final reports as to how renewal periods have gone for congregations, we often hear that congregations have gained increased confidence in their own people and their own community's ability to pursue mission—which actually allows them to freely appreciate their pastor even more! Healthy, self-reliant congregations and healthy, refreshed pastors are a winning combination for ministry.

As Melissa Bane Sevier says about pastors, "Every time we [pastors] encourage our congregations to think we are essential to their well-being, we do them and us a great disservice... [S]abbatical can give the distance to restore a healthy relationship."[4]

You know that the congregation is on the right track in the process when the questions gradually change from, "Will the congregation survive?" to, "What can we do in this renewal period to help the congregation thrive?"

---

[4]Melissa Bane Sevier, *Journeying Toward Renewal: A Spiritual Companion for Pastoral Sabbaticals* (Bethesda, Md.: Alban Institute, 2002), 62.

4. Will the Pastor Leave If They Go on Sabbatical?

Many congregation members fear that, if the pastor steps away from the congregation, they might discern a call to leave. This is a valid fear, especially if (as I *don't* recommend) the sabbatical is a means of escape or taking a break between the pastor and the congregation, a "trial separation," as it were.

But if we remember that sabbatical leaves are for healthy pastors in healthy congregations, then we can rest easy. The pastor should be doing this because they want to be refreshed for ministry *in* the congregation, and the congregation should see this experience as an investment in its shared future with the pastor. Obviously, situations come up in which pastors who have gone on sabbatical are called to move on; however, these should be the exception rather than the rule.[5]

I recommend that pastors who are considering undertaking this process with their congregations signify (publicly, and perhaps even in writing) their intention to remain in their congregations for at least a year following the leave; sometimes even two or three years. This is not about legalism or restrictions; the intent is positive. Pastors agreeing to remain in the congregation after the sabbatical leave are demonstrating that they understand the sabbatical to be a part of a total congregational endeavor, meant to strengthen (among other things) the relationship between the pastor and the congregation for the long haul.

Common Concerns from Pastors

Believe it or not, sometimes the pastor is the harder "sell" when it comes to taking time away from the congregation, even if that

---

[5]And, of course, in some church traditions, such as with Methodists and Roman Catholics, clergy might have very little control over when and where they are assigned.

time is intentionally structured for renewal! The following are some of the most common concerns that we have found that pastors have when contemplating renewal leaves.

1. Will the Church Fall Apart without Me?

A highly successful pastor of a large African American Church in South Carolina was in love with ministry, but had been through enough intense turmoil that his body and heart were crying out for a chance to be away and regroup. He spent nights in prayer considering the possibility of a sabbatical, and at one point in the prayer he cried out to God, "God, I can't take time away from my church!" As he tells it, the answer came back: "No, but you can take time away from Mine!"

Pastors are very important shepherds of their congregations. But, as stated above, a healthy congregation will know first and foremost that it belongs to God, and also that its heart and soul lies with the vocation of every member, not just the pastor.

Now, again, when it comes to the question of timing, if the congregation is in conflict, or unstable, or is otherwise not in a steady season, then it is *not* the right time to undertake a renewal period. Other kinds of work (prayer, consulting, relationship-building, etc.) needs to happen before the pastor can be away. But if the congregation is in a stable place and looking to be both refreshed in its energy and brought to the next level of mission, then a renewal leave will (as noted above) potentially unlock ministry potential within the congregation that can best flourish during a time when the pastor is temporarily away.

2. Will the Congregation Have Conflict while I Am Away?

Most congregations (particularly those who do not have multiple pastors on staff) whose pastors go on sabbatical contract with supply preachers to cover worship (and perhaps sacraments) while they are away. In many cases, these supply pastors also provide some pastoral care to congregation members during these months. In many cases, these pastors can help coordinate proper responses to congregational conflict if and when it arises.

However, the most successful renewal leaves proceed on the assumption that, while some amount of congregational conflict is to be expected, for the most part the congregation will be healthy enough to handle issues that arise in a faithful and respectful manner, tabling any serious discussions until the pastor returns and the congregation and pastor can tackle the issue together.

3. What If a Pastoral Emergency Arises?

Life in congregations does not slow to a stop while the pastor is away on leave. Even if the leave is taken during a slower season in the congregation's life (say, summertime), pastoral issues will almost certainly arise. Key members may pass away. Baptisms and other life milestones will occur.

While circumstances might arise forcing pastors to cut their leaves short in order to attend to a congregational emergency, one of the most important things a congregation can do to prepare itself for the renewal period is to put structures in place to cover emergencies without bringing the pastor who is on sabbatical in—and then commit to following them!

One of the key ingredients of a successful renewal experience is a formal plan, worked out between the pastor and the congregation, to ensure limited contact between the congregation and the pastor while the pastor is away. The more thoroughly "away" the pastor can be during the leave, the more the benefits of the renewal for both the pastor and the congregation can come into fruition. If the pastor spends large parts of the leave thinking about/intervening in the congregation, then they can never quite get the full benefits of focus on renewal activities. Meanwhile, the congregation can inadvertently be taught that members themselves are not empowered to respond to ministry challenges when they arise. This is not good.

Pastors and congregations should go into the leave experience assuming that the pastor will have very little contact with parishioners during the leave—even in cases such as deaths or other pastoral emergencies. Congregations and pastors should trust their people, and not undertake the renewal experience absent that trust. But if the trust that the congregation and other staff (permanent or interim) can handle emergencies is there, then everyone's mind will be at ease. The work of the church belongs to the whole people; this is a prime opportunity to embody that as a congregation.

Two more notes about communication...

First, in this social media age, most pastors will post on Facebook or blog or do other such things as they pursue their renewal activities. How can we expect a pastor and family to be at the Grand Canyon or a French cathedral and not post pictures? The main thing to avoid, though, is pastors communicating in real time with congregation members.

To give an example: Posting on social media is asynchronous—that is, pastors do not have to be "on" in real time in order to post their pictures and thoughts. That is okay. What is less okay is, say, a pastor video-conferencing into worship, since that sort of synchronous contact would force the pastor to be back "on" as pastor of the congregation during that video call. If a congregation is going to engage with a pastor's pictures, posts, blog articles, etc., it should be done asynchronously on their own time, and with minimal real-time interaction with the pastor. Moreover, the pastor should have freedom to respond or not, with no congregational expectations around how immediate or extensive the responses are. The pastor should be freed from real-time engagement with the congregation in order to focus on renewal time and activities.

Second, pastors should avoid bringing members of the congregation along on renewal activities, even if those members are also friends. If the congregation is present, even in the form of just a few people, then the pastor is not truly "away" from the congregation and in a space of deep renewal. Moreover, a congregation's support for a pastor's renewal program should not depend on members being able to go along on activities as well; the congregation should have its own activities about which it is enthusiastic.

4. Have I Been in Ministry Long Enough?

Some denominations or congregations have policies as to how long a pastor needs to be at a congregation before being eligible for a sabbatical; often, it is a period of about seven years or so. Those policies are fine, although—continuing what was said above—we should note that the congregation should not assume that just because a pastor is "due" a sabbatical that it is the right time in the life of the pastor or the congregation for the renewal period to happen. If the pastor is due a sabbatical based on congregational policy, but either the pastor or congregation is not in a healthy enough place for both to be at ease while the pastor is away, then it is not a good idea.

But the reverse is also true: it may be the case that it is the right time in the life of the pastor and the congregation at some time other than seven years in. In the grants program I direct, we award sabbatical grants to congregations to support pastors at all stages in their careers: a few years in, midway, or even a few years from retirement. A sabbatical when the pastor is still early in ministry can help them focus priorities on what they want to achieve in the main portions of their career. A leave taken midway through the pastor's career can restore energy and help the pastor recommit to the work they have undertaken for the long term. Time away when the pastor is a few years from retirement can help that pastor "finish strong," and can also be a powerful way for a congregation to honor the pastor's years of service.

As with so many things related to sabbatical, there is no fixed "right time"; all depends on the process of deep discussion and discernment between the pastor and the congregation as to whether the timing is right for them.

5. Does It Really Have to Be Several Months?

My strong recommendation is that the pastor be away for no less than three months. In 20 years of work granting sabbatical leave grants to congregations, the Lilly Endowment Clergy Renewal Programs have demonstrated that it takes at least three months for the pastor to enter into the "rhythm" of sabbatical, have quality time away, and then ease into reentry. Some pastors take four months, and some as many as six months. That decision depends upon your congregation's preferences, but a sabbatical of less than three months will not be as valuable as it could be.

Meanwhile, renewal periods of less than three months run the risk of seeming like an extended vacation rather than an intentional time of renewal. It may be intimidating (or perhaps even seem extravagant) to picture being away that long, but it is one of the best ways for both the pastor and the congregation to signify that they understand that the pastor's renewal leave is not a vacation but rather an intentional time of refocusing for ministry. What might seem like an abundance in fact indicates focus and seriousness; renewal takes time and gentle rhythm, and should not be rushed.

In all these cases, I need to stress again that the work spent gaining buy-in across your congregation is time very well spent, and should not be rushed. Some congregations are used to the idea of pastoral sabbatical and will be ready to support it right away; in other cases, it might take months or even years for your congregation to become fully acclimated to the idea. But the work that you do in getting the widest possible base of support from the congregation will not only lead to a better experience for both the pastor and the congregation during the renewal period, but it will also lay the groundwork for subsequent pastors to engage their congregation in renewal opportunities as well.

3

What Should the Pastor Do during the Renewal Period?

Picture your congregation three months from now. The pastor walks into their office feeling ready to go: energized, spiritually rooted, and creatively inspired. The congregation, similarly, feels as if it has gotten a new injection of energy and insight. The question is: What would have been happening in the three months prior to get pastor and congregation to that state? What would work for you all to get yourselves there?

Don't think about what another congregation or pastor did. Don't think about what you think "should" be involved. Go deep into the questions for yourselves: What would get your pastor and your congregation to that place of renewed energy? What activities? What destinations? What practices?? Who should come along to share in the experiences? What would work for *you*?

No two pastors will answer this alike. All sorts of people enter into the ministry: introverts, extroverts, sports fans, artists, amateur athletes, historians, bookworms. They may be single or married, young or old. The question, "What will renew my spirit for ministry?" has as many answers as there are pastors.

Similarly, no two congregations are identical. Congregations may benefit most from bringing in speakers and guest preachers during the leave. Or, they might appreciate activities centered on telling faith stories of members, or engaging in intense study of biblical texts. Maybe the congregation will have a large celebration, or maybe the experience will be low key. Don't worry about what other congregations or pastors are doing. What will work best for *you*?

This chapter includes some tips to consider as you and your pastor think about putting together the most beneficial shared renewal experience. In addition to what follows, pastors can consult some excellent resources for planning sabbatical leaves: Richard Bullock and Richard Bruesehoff's *Clergy Renewal: The Alban Guide to Sabbatical Planning* and Melissa Bane Sevier's *Journeying Toward Renewal: A Spiritual Companion for Pastoral Sabbaticals* have been used quite successfully by a number of pastors.

The Most Important Distinction: Joy vs. Obligation

When the pastor chooses activities for their sabbatical, the main question to ask is: Are the activities that the pastor is proposing to do chosen out of joy or out of obligation?

Consider a pastor who wants to spend a renewal leave researching and writing a small book on a hero of the faith—say, John Wesley. Now, the question is: Is this pastor proposing to do this because Wesley is truly inspirational for the pastor? Does time seem to disappear whenever the pastor is deep in reading Wesley's writings, or when the pastor is reflecting in writing on Wesley's life? Does the pastor draw energy and calm from this work?

Or, is the pastor feeling secretly guilty (or secretly pressured, whether that pressure is real or not) and wants to come back from the leave having some achievement in hand in order to demonstrate that the sabbatical was worth it? Is someone expecting the pastor to be like Moses and descend from the mountain with "golden tablets" of completed manuscripts or new preaching insights or visibly sharpened skills? Did the writing happen under deadline rather than with luxurious freedom to go slowly and deliberate and meditate?

In both cases, the pastor might return with a book on Wesley. But in the second case, the "sabbatical" was really just the same pressures of work in a different setting. Deadlines, expectations, worry about justifying the time—these are the realities that often turn research and writing into obligation rather than joy.

But in the first case, what might have been work to some was bliss to the pastor. Writing projects on sabbaticals are easy test cases for the joy vs. obligation question: Are there deadlines, or is part of the spiritual reconnection coming from the unhurried pace? Did the pastor choose the topic because they think it will appeal to others, or does it speak directly to their intellectual curiosity and hunger? Is the end product, or the process itself, at the forefront in the pastor's description of the sabbatical?

The same goes for pastors who go on sabbatical to take on new skills. For instance, is a pastor who wants to start to learn Spanish on the sabbatical doing so because something about the language and the doors that it opens speaks directly to their heart for ministry, or because they are under pressure to start a Spanish-speaking worship service? Is the pastor who wants to travel the country and experience noted preachers in action on Sunday morning doing so because it fires their passion for God's word and the pulpit, or because they have been subtly getting feedback that makes them think they need a sabbatical to improve their preaching? Is the pastor traveling to the Holy Land because they truly want to see it or because they think it is a sufficiently "religious" trip to where it will help sell the sabbatical to the congregation? All of these are instances of why it is crucial to apply the joy vs. obligation test to every significant activity on the proposed agenda for the pastor's sabbatical. If an activity is chosen because it will bring joy, then it is the right activity; but even the "right" activity becomes wrong if joy gives way to obligation or pressure!

This is not to say that learning while on sabbatical leave is wrong. Far from it! It is okay for the pastor to want to learn more about an intriguing topic, increase skill at listening or preaching or pastoral care, build houses for Habitat for Humanity, or to otherwise undertake things that might look like "work" to other pastors or congregation members, *as long as* these activities speak deeply to the enthusiasm and soul of the pastor. If an activity is done out of joy and not obligation, then virtually any activity can be appropriate for a sabbatical leave.[1]

One note: Many pastors may want to spend sabbatical doing missionary-type work (such as building wells in Africa or teaching at a denominational seminary in Korea) because they have a deep heart for mission and doing so would pass the joy vs. obligation test. In most cases, this is fine, but a pastor should avoid traveling to work on behalf of a mission with which their congregation has a formal partnership. The reason is because doing so will cause the pastor to reassume their formal role as pastor of the congregation, even if they are thousands of miles away. Pastors wanting to do mission work on the sabbatical should pick an organization with which their congregation has no formal ties so that they can truly be "civilians" and not ambassadors for their congregations as they pursue the work.

---

[1]In general, sabbaticals should also not be used solely for the pursuit of formal academic degrees, such as the Doctor of Ministry. The formal and product-oriented nature of these degree programs makes them valuable as continued education, but ill-suited for renewal in the sense that we are using it here.

Bucket List or Energy Balance?

A mistake that many pastors going on sabbatical for the first time make is to pack too many activities into the time period. This is understandable—for many pastors, sabbatical (particularly if it is funded by the congregation or a grant) is a rare opportunity, and pastors will want to take full advantage of the time and resources. But—and this is crucial—the goals of a renewal leave (revitalization, renewal of rootedness in call, slow growth in spiritual connectedness, etc.) all depend upon a deliberate pace with lots of "downtime" for reflection and processing built in. You don't want a situation in which the pastor comes back needing a vacation after the sabbatical!

The key is to put together a three or four month program that contains, not only a variety of activities, but a balance of energy. High-intensity periods (such as foreign travel) should be followed by periods of downtime for processing, recuperation, etc. If you are a pastor contemplating sabbatical, give up the idea that you will be able to hit everything on your life's bucket list. Think instead of crafting a focused series of activities that will allow you to experience unhurried, unscheduled rejuvenation at various points during the leave. Have adventure, but breathe. Don't wait until you get back to process; find times to process and muse along the way. This will maximize your energy for reentry when the time comes to return to the congregation.

Now, what "downtime" looks like depends greatly on the individual. For some people, downtime means a book on a quiet beach; for others, it means rock climbing. Some people are born travelers and do it with ease; for others travel is automatically a high-energy endeavor. Forget what other pastors have done; you should lay out the range of activities that speak most deeply to you, and then honestly assess (based on your own knowledge of your energy expenditure style) whether the program is too much or just right.

Don't try to fill up your bucket list; find the balance of intensity and rest that will have you returning to the congregation fired up and ready to take on a new season of ministry with new energy.

Should There Be a Theme?

Some pastors like to have a theme to their sabbatical, such as "Improvisation" or "Community in the 21st Century." In the first chapter we heard about pastors who chose hospitality and the theology of C.S. Lewis as guiding themes. One pastor, an avid quilter, proposed (along with her congregation) a "Weaving the Stories of Our Lives" theme that had her searching out rare fabrics while meditating on the way in which her personal narratives wove in with that of biblical characters. Another pastor returned to his home country of Korea to meditate on the role that origins play in our destinies, so a theme of "Roots and Branches" was appropriate for his journey.

If a theme is helpful, then choose one that speaks to you and let it orient your choices of activities. But don't let the theme become a constraint. I know a number of pastors who had very successful sabbatical leaves whose activities did not fit together into any sort of coherent theme. In those cases, what all of the activities *did* have in common was that they all spoke to different aspects of the pastors' souls and vocations; it was clear that they and their loved ones would benefit from each one of the activities.

So while a good theme can help organize thoughts about what the pastor and congregation might want to achieve during the renewal period, don't let the tail wag the dog. If a theme is helpful, use it; but if the only theme is, "All of these activities will be very renewing," then that is enough. One of the best sabbatical leaves I ever heard about was that of an Orthodox priest who split his time between meditating at a monastery for a month, pursuing his deeply spiritual avocation of antique book-binding for another month, and then spending the last month getting his amateur pilot's license so as to meditate on viewing the earth from a "God's eye" view! The three activities together energized different areas of his person and work, and no further theme was necessary.

Who Should Come?

As Christians, none of us pursues our discipleship alone. We follow Jesus Christ as part of a network of life-giving relationships. Our very identities as family members, workers in the Kingdom, and church members are woven together with others. This means that, for both pastors and congregations, renewing the soul often means spending intentional time feeding relationships that are meaningful to us.

As we have already discussed, the families of pastors are often the ones who bear the brunt of the irregularity of pastoral schedules. Provided that funds and timing work out, many pastors choose to involve family members for at least part of their sabbaticals. One pastor, reflecting back on his leave several years later, remarked that the most transformative part of the experience was that his family sat down and ate every meal together for five months! Other pastors talk about being able to provide experiences for their partners and children that could not happen apart from a focused time of travel.

That said, some pastors benefit from a mix of intensive family time and solo time spent in meditation, prayer, travel, etc. Lots of different combinations are possible—for instance, two weeks of solo prayer and journaling time in the woods, followed by a month of travel with the family, then ending with solo trips to see mentors, or taking a class. In my observation, such mixes are common, especially since it is likely that family members and children will have work/school obligations that may limit travel time.

As mentioned above, pastors should avoid traveling with congregation members. There are grey areas here—sometimes pastors are good friends with their congregants, and a pastor might envision, say, taking a fishing buddy from the congregation on a fishing trip as part of the leave. But the problem is that if *anyone* from the congregation comes along, then the pastor is automatically "on" as pastor. The most effective sabbatical leaves are the ones during which the pastor can have genuine separation from the congregation so as to be able to come back ready for deeper connection; if the pastor is too connected to congregation members, even friends, during that time, then that process can be short-circuited.

Other friends, though, can be powerful companions on leaves as well. If a pastor is unmarried, they might not wish to travel alone, and can choose to bring friends, seminary classmates, or others who are and have been meaningful companions in forming the pastor. As with so much else, the choice of who comes should be determined on a case-by-case basis, and in consultation between the pastor and the congregation.

Planning vs. Spontaneity

How much planning should go into a renewal leave? Does too much planning threaten the spontaneity and relaxation that many pastors hope to achieve during their sabbatical periods?

We can best answer that with an analogy. To casual listeners, jazz music often sounds like pure improvisation. Talented soloists will take off on saxophone or piano jazz solos, creating irreplaceable moments of spontaneous creation, and the audience might assume that the music was mostly a happy accident of chaos coalescing into form. However, knowledgeable fans will know that most jazz music is anything but pure spontaneity; in fact, in order to achieve the freedom to improvise with excellence, jazz musicians must practice with deep rigor the chord changes, structure, and inner musical logic of a given tune. First comes the firm blueprint, then comes the joyous deviation from it.

Or, picture an excellent sermon. In many cases, some of the most powerful moments of a given sermon or speech might be spontaneous or unplanned (such as the most famous lines of Dr. Martin Luther King Jr.'s "I Have a Dream" speech); however, such moments of improvisation, going "off script," depend on there having been a solid script in the first place. Plans give orientation and direction; it is once they have been lived into that they can be launching pads for pleasant surprises.

So too with sabbatical plans. It is true that, once the rhythm of sabbatical has been achieved, many pastors revel in unplanned detours, surprises, or other deviations from the original "script" of the leave. However, these are usually only beneficial if they take place within the framework of a clear plan that will ensure that such practical considerations as budget, time constraints, the travel needs of sabbatical companions, etc., are not scuttled by opportunities as they arise.

This suggests that as much planning as possible should go into the activities and the logistics surrounding them: costs, timelines, etc. "We'll go to Ireland and then just see what happens..." As charming as it may sound, this kind of attitude actually risks diminishing the benefits of sabbatical by making pastors and their families more vulnerable to contingencies and logistical hassles that can be avoided with enough foresight. My advice to pastors is to err on the side of overplanning, and then you can be comfortable improvising once you are actually "on the ground" on the leave.

The best way to outline a sabbatical is to account for every day within basic blocks of time—e.g., "two weeks in Wisconsin reading monastic literature," followed by "four days visiting family in Michigan," "three weeks in Sweden hiking with college roommates," etc. This provides structure and helps with budget planning, communication logistics, etc. It has the added bonus of helping the congregation follow along with the pastor and tailor its activities, as desired, to those of the pastor at any given time—not to mention praying for the pastor and any companions as they travel to each new area!

―――――――――――

Although itineraries for the pastoral sabbatical portions of the renewal period can and should be individually tailored, the principles mention in this chapter apply across the board. Aim for joy and not obligation, plus energy balance over sheer quantity of activities; bring along loved ones separate from your congregation; and plan it well enough that inevitable contingencies and unexpected events will not derail your ability to meet your goals.

Most of all...*dream*. Breathe. Give yourself over to the vulnerability of showing the world what it is that feeds your soul, and trust your congregation to want that for you. That trust is the cornerstone of sabbaticals that renew *and* delight.

4

What Should the Congregation Do during the Renewal Period?

As you can already tell, if there is one message that I want you to take from this book, it is this: renewal periods are about more than the pastor's activities on sabbatical. Renewal, if it is to be maximally successful, is a shared endeavor between the pastor and the congregation.

The specifics of what this shared work looks like will, again, vary from congregation to congregation, but in this chapter we will examine some strategies that have worked for different congregations, as well as answer some commonly asked questions about congregational activities while the pastor is away on sabbatical leave.

What Resources Does the Congregation Need?

In order to successfully take on a renewal period, the congregation needs funds set aside for that purpose. The funds needed can be broken down into a few different categories:

Salary: During the pastor's sabbatical, the pastor should continue to be paid the exact same salary and benefits as when they are present in the congregation. The pastor is not on unpaid leave; the pastor is engaging in the "work" of renewal, and the pastor's compensation for this work should not be any different.

Money for Supply Staff: In a congregation with only one pastor, that pastor's leaving for a sabbatical will likely necessitate that the congregation hire a supply pastor to cover worship, preaching, and basic pastoral care needs during the three-to-four–month period. Congregations should be sure to take mileage, honoraria, and remuneration into account when constructing the budget for this pastor. In congregations with multiple pastors or other situations in which no extra staff are needed, a congregation might still consider giving stipends or bonuses to staff who will almost inevitably take on added duties while the pastor is away.

Money for Other Congregational Activities: As we will discuss below, congregations can use the time while the pastor is away to explore their own passions for ministry, which many congregations will link thematically to the pastor's activities. Many of these activities might be free, but some might require funding. Also, many congregations have found that it is helpful to have a "sending" celebration and a "reunion" celebration at the beginning and end of the pastor's sabbatical; these celebrations should also be a planned part of the congregation's overall renewal budget.

Assistance for the Pastor's Activities: Depending on the context and the nature of the pastor's activities, congregations may choose to help supplement the cost of the pastor's activities, or not. Depending on how the congregation chooses to finance the renewal period (see below), most congregations will choose to help with these expenses at some level.

When Should Renewal Happen, and How Does a Congregation Pay for It?

There are a number of strategies that congregations can use to fund renewal periods for their pastors and themselves. Absent a large single donor, the two most common ways are to write a yearly amount to be put into the congregation's sabbatical fund as part of the annual budget, and/or to seek grant funding.

Regarding savings: It is increasingly common for pastors to request that sabbatical savings be a part of their contract with congregations. Every year, as part of the pastor's remuneration, the congregation will deposit a set amount into a fund that is then available for use when the congregation and the pastor are ready. This usually happens as part of a larger sabbatical policy in the congregation, in which, say, every seven years the pastor is eligible for a congregation-supported sabbatical. Having this as a line item in the congregational budget each year can not only help the congregation save in a disciplined fashion for the renewal period, but it can also provide a tangible reminder to the congregation about commitment to renewal and support for shared ministry that is part of the congregation's ethos.

A note on timing: There's no doubt that sabbatical policies in congregations can be very helpful. The only caveat to remember is that, if the renewal is to be maximally beneficial for the pastor and the congregation, then consideration as to the right timing has to be about more than whether the pastor is "due" a sabbatical. If seven years have elapsed but the congregation is, say, in the middle of a major building project, then the pastor should consider delaying the leave until the project is completed. Similarly, if the congregation is experiencing significant conflict or upheaval, then waiting can also be a good idea.

I don't say that lightly, for, if pastors are counting on a sabbatical after a certain amount of time but the anticipated sabbatical timing hits at an inopportune time in the life of the pastor or congregation, it can be painful or frustrating to wait. However, the dividends paid by a properly timed sabbatical (as opposed to one that is simply "due") are valuable enough that they make waiting until the right time a benefit to both the pastor and the congregation.

Regarding grant funding: Congregations in the United States can apply for grants to several foundations whose work supports congregational life in U.S. Christianity. The Lilly Endowment Clergy Renewal Programs (administered by Christian Theological Seminary in Indianapolis, Indiana) give grants of up to $50,000 to up to 150 congregations per year to support their pastors taking a three-to-four–month renewal leave; up to $15,000 of those funds can be used by the congregation to cover costs and pursue congregational activities while the pastor is away.[1] For pastors who wish to spend their sabbaticals pursuing a focused project, the Louisville Institute offers Pastoral Study Project grants of up to $15,000 for pastors to "investigate issues related to the Christian life of faith, North American religious practices and institutions, and/or major challenges facing contemporary society."[2]

These grants can, of course, really help with funding renewal activities. But, if possible, the congregation should put plans in place so that the renewal is not fully dependent upon receiving a grant. The application process for these grants is highly competitive, so even congregations with well-constructed renewal leave plans may not receive grant funding in a given

---

[1]For more information on these programs, see www.lillyclergyrenewal.org.

[2]For more information, visit https://louisville-institute.org/programs-grants-and-fellowships/grants/pastoral-study-project/.

year. If it is important that a renewal leave happen at a certain point in time, it is helpful if the congregation can have a backup source of funding in place if grant funding is not secured. Be creative, both with what the congregation might do with extensive financial resources *and* with limited ones; sometimes, the creativity of making funds stretch produces its own kind of rewards.

What Kinds of Activities Can the Congregation Do?

As is the case with pastoral activities, congregations should not worry about what they hear other congregations doing during their pastor's sabbatical. Your congregation is unique, and the life history and social setting of your members come together to form a community unlike any other. This means that, as with pastors, conversations about this uniqueness and what feeds the soul of the people in that place can be incredibly valuable in and of themselves. Most congregations have regular conversations about mission, identity, growth strategies, etc., but when was the last time your congregation had an unhurried, open conversation about what things give it life?

This is the joy of renewal periods—they are gloriously super-fluous. By refusing to serve the immediate, they open space for the deep and expansive. They are not designed first and foremost to be congregational strategy sessions about worship design, church growth, financial matters, etc. Just as, while on sabbatical, the pastor is invited to step away from the day-to-day demands of ministry and leadership in order to focus deeply on spiritual matters, so too the renewal period can be a time for the congregation to indulge in the blessed luxury of asking questions about joy and meaning.

Now, in saying this I do not mean to go against what I said before about how congregational leaders might also pick up some leadership tasks while the pastor is away! But the truth is that the two emphases—greater congregational leadership *and* deeper time for exploring questions of what gives life to the congregation—are not actually opposed. The former can draw out the latter, and vice versa.

A congregation whose pastor was on sabbatical instituted a lay preaching series to help cover the pulpit while the pastor was away. One by one, various leaders and faithful members of the congregation shared testimony during the sermon time about the operations of God's grace in their lives. As the series continued, the congregation realized that the intense focus on new programs and added activities in the last few years had, inadvertently, served to clutter some of the core reasons why people chose to go to church there—personal connections, unhurried worship, clear focus on the gospel.

The congregation taking on more "preaching to itself," as it were, served to create a space in which eventually the people had the courage to take a pause and begin to engage in what C. Christopher Smith and John Pattison call "slow church"— the careful, connectional, simple realities of life together in community apart from busy-ness and pressure to grow.[3] So increased leadership and increased reflection can go hand in hand.

The best congregational activities during a renewal period, then, are the ones that draw on and enhance these twin goods: encouraging leadership among congregation members while also creating space for reflection.

---

[3]C. Christopher Smith and John Pattison, *Slow Church: Cultivating Community in the Patient Way of Jesus* (Downers Grove, Ill.: Intervarsity Press, 2014).

Some congregations (such as the one discussed in the Introduction) bring in guest speakers and preachers to focus on topics of interest to the congregation—especially if those topics relate somehow to the theme of the pastor's sabbatical leave. Depending on the congregation's finances, it can draw on local colleges, seminaries, or other educational institutions for speakers. Most seminary professors and professors at Christian colleges in particular are eager to speak in congregational settings. Be sure to allocate money in the total renewal period to pay a fair mileage rate and honorarium.

Don't assume that the most profound topics will be the most "religious," or vice versa. Sometimes, congregations have gotten more out of bringing in experts to talk about ecology, science, art, or health care than would have happened had they brought in theologians! Just as some of the most theologically rich sabbaticals consist of "non-church" activities that nonetheless draw the pastor deep into the joy of God's creation, so too sometimes congregations can have their imaginations for ministry fired by topics that at first seem irrelevant to ministry, but soon show themselves to be deeply resonant with the lives of the people.

Again, have the frank conversation about what is on the hearts of the people in the congregation, and don't be afraid to craft a plan that might make no sense to a neighboring congregation, but for *your* people is fitted and right.

Things to Avoid

As the congregation thinks about its activities, its imagination should range far and wide. However, there are several categories of activity that should be avoided by congregations during the renewal period.

First, while the pastor is away, the congregation should not hire consultants or bring in speakers/facilitators who will cause the congregation to start having conversations that are best had while the pastor is present. While conversations about theology, mission, Bible, history, culture, etc., can be very profitable for congregations to discuss while the pastor is gone, if talks turn to finances, staffing, outreach, or other sensitive matters, then the congregation might find itself embroiled in controversies that can spin out of control. Do not bring in "stewardship experts" or "church growth strategists" or others whose talks are likely to set off debates about sensitive matter such as money, attendance, and staff performance/compensation.

Some congregations make the mistake of thinking of the time when the pastor is gone as akin to an interim period between pastors, which is a time when congregations are called to be introspective about both mission *and* ministry details. Renewal periods are not that; they are times for introspection about mission, but not for detail work around financial and operational matters. Let the renewal period be a time to focus on spiritual, theological, and recreational matters; this will, as with the pastor, give the congregation fresh energy and insight to tackle practicalities once the pastor and congregation are reunited.

Meanwhile, if the congregation has secured grant funding or donations for renewal activities during the sabbatical, then make sure that the money goes toward activities and not capital improvements to the building or grounds. A congregation who uses the renewal period to focus on, say, Celtic spirituality has the potential for a very meaningful time; however, if that same congregation were to use funds set aside for renewal to build at multi-thousand dollar labyrinth on the church grounds, it might be hard to avoid the impression that the labyrinth itself (or the augmented sound system, or the patched roof, etc.) was the real point of the renewal. Focus on experiences, not property.

———————

As with the pastor's activities, the congregation should not feel bound by a theme. If a theme is helpful, then use it; however, it may be that the best way for the congregation and the pastor to both have powerful experiences during the renewal period is for each to chart an individual course, so as to marvel at the ways God can make the courses converge once reunion happens.

5

How Do Renewal Leaves Bring Us into God's Mission?

As we come to the end of this book, it is time to ask the most important question: "Why even do this?" And that answer comes down to, for me, that of another question: "How does undertaking this process bring congregations closer to the heart of God's mission? How does the process of renewal relate to what God calls all of us in our congregations to do?"

Praise of the People

There is ample testimony in both the Bible and the Judeo-Christian tradition that, when we are engaged in Sabbath, when we are engaged in intentional rest and renewal, we are in fact close to the heart of the faith itself.

In the Old Testament, proper keeping of the sabbatical was central to Israel's identity and its testimony that the God of Israel is also the God over all things. The one who calls us to work on behalf of the orphan, the widow, and the stranger is also the one who invites us into a period of rest and praise (see, for instance, Ex. 20:8–11). In the New Testament, Jesus regularly withdraws from the work of public ministry in order to re-center himself in prayer—including in the Garden of Gethsemane, just prior to his taking on the most intense work of salvation and justice for humankind.

Sabbath and generosity, abundance and justice, are not separate, and this is a key theological point. *Because* God is the God of abundance who calls us into feeling that God is enough, we are formed ourselves for the ministry of sharing God's bounty with those who are victims of the sinful structures of scarcity that we humans are so good at creating.

If this is at all true, then rest and justice are equal and intertwined modes of how pastors and their congregations might respond to the call to be about the work of proclamation and justice in the world.

Heart Song

When I became the director of the Lilly Endowment Clergy Renewal Programs in 2012, I inherited (in addition to the usual policies and procedures) the tagline to the programs: "What will make your heart sing?"

Being a somewhat somber sort (theologically and otherwise), I admit that I struggled with that tagline at first. It seemed a bit...*sentimental*. Florid, even. Out of keeping with the lofty and serious goals that I ascribed to the programs. There is so much oversentimentalized talk of "the heart" in Christian circles that my natural suspicion as to how profound the phrase could really be kicked in.

But I have come around, and I can say why.

Remember the tableau we set up in a previous chapter, and the question that we asked in regards to it: "Picture your congregation three months from now. The pastor walks into their office feeling ready to go: energized, spiritually rooted, and creatively inspired. The congregation, similarly, feels as if it has gotten a new injection of energy and insight. The question is: What would have been happening in the three months prior to get pastor and congregation to that state? What would work for you all to get yourselves there?"

The answer to that question is, as we have discussed, highly individual for pastors and congregations alike—no two would answer it the same way. And that is the beauty of the renewal programs—they encourage variety. Some pastors travel the world with their families. Some go deeply into their studies and read and write for pleasure instead of deadlines. Some make art, or take on new physical and spiritual practices. Some bring along spouses and partners; others bring along seminary classmates and friends. The variety in sabbatical planning is as vast as the variety within ministry itself, and, indeed, to ask a question about the heart (What are the hopes and dreams that fuel pastors as people and as proclaimers of the gospel? What gives shape to the unique people that make up every congregation?) is an intimate and sacred invitation. As I said from the outset, congregations that have the courage to answer the invitation on behalf of themselves and their pastors are deeply honoring their pastors by doing so—and, in so doing, are creating a culture of honor within the congregation itself.

Pastors and congregations undertaking renewal leaves are invited to engage in the life-giving activities that will allow them to carry forward their shared mission together in ways that far exceed simple recreation. We can even go so far as to say that the embodied action of sabbatical, of rest for the sake of renewal, is conformity to Christ—it is one of the ways in which we follow in the footsteps of Jesus. As Wayne Muller writes, commenting on Jesus' healing ministry:

Jesus did not wait until everyone had been properly cared for, until all who sought him had healed. He did not ask permission to go, nor did he leave anyone behind "on call," or even let his disciples know where he was going. Jesus obeyed a deeper rhythm. When the moment for rest had come, the time for healing was over. He would simply stop, retire to a quiet place, and pray... When Jesus prayed he was at rest, nourished by the healing spirit that saturates those still, quiet places.[1]

Do pastors "work" on sabbatical? Do congregations do a particular kind of work while they pursue their renewal activities? Here we see a deeply theological point. The "work" of Sabbath is discipline, wise discernment, and a letting go in order to trust in God's abundance. It is a theologically intense and missionally powerful act, one by which the congregation honors the pastor and the pastor rededicates themselves to service in the congregation. Renewal work is work that proceeds from trust in God and God's abundance.

Heart songs are diverse and varied, and many of them have the sort of gritty edge that is characteristic of actual truth-telling as opposed to treacle. Parish ministry in the 21st century is a challenging reality on economic, political, and spiritual fronts. No superficial song can reach the ears of pastors and congregations that seek spiritual solace in a world that seems torn apart by noise and discordance. We have so many distractions, and in an era in which the church is changing so rapidly, it can be hard to get our spiritual bearings.

The promise of the gospel tells us that we are worth more than the sum of our works. However, those of us who spend time in

---

[1]Wayne Muller, *Sabbath: Finding Rest, Renewal, and Delight in Our Busy Lives* (New York: Bantam, 1999), 25.

congregations know how vulnerable congregations themselves are to being lulled into the idea that it is more busy-ness, more programs, more work that will somehow make the congregation viable and prosperous.

The antidote to this is dreaming—not the dreams that lull us into complacency, or the fantasies that draw us from reality, but a different kind of dreaming.

What sort of dreams? Dreams of heart song. Dreams of relationships with spouses and loved ones restored, physical and spiritual health gained, creativity awakened, gratitude for a life spent in ministry rekindled. Congregations, too, dream of honoring pastors with sabbatical opportunities, and receiving a renewed pastor who brings fresh vigor. Both pastors and congregations can dream of what is possible when the heart for ministry is fed and mobilized.

Dreams, of course, are sacred and often fragile things. Indeed, amidst the mechanics of the grant management on our end, the staff of Clergy Renewal are regularly struck by what a delicate and precious thing it is to hold dreams. "What will make your heart sing?" is, I have come to believe, such an intimate question – all the more so for pertaining to deep matters of faith, life-giving relationships, and a renewal of inspiration for the calling to public ministry. The longer I observe congregations holding these conversations, the more I am in awe of God's work in that space – the work of holding space for personal spirituality, celebration of congregational innovation and courage, and astonishment at the creativity by which God's spirit continually shapes and reshapes the landscape of ministry across the country.

When we are astonished, we are gratified; and when we are gratified, we are free for mission. We do not pursue work in

God's vineyard with the frenzy of scarcity, thinking that we must carve out worth for ourselves or relevance for our churches by means of our actions. Instead, we act freely and nimbly as ministers of God's abundance, seeking out the places where our hands and our proclamation can let that divine plenty be felt and seen by those who hunger.

Abundance and Ministry

Abraham Joshua Heschel writes, in his classic book on Sabbath-keeping:

> He who wants to enter the holiness of the day must first lay down the profanity of clattering commerce, of being yoked to toil. He must go away from the screech of dissonant days, from the nervousness and fury of acquisitiveness and the betrayal in embezzling his own life. He must say farewell to manual work and learn to understand that the world has already been created and will survive without the help of man. Six days a week we wrestle with the world, wringing profit from the earth; on the Sabbath we especially care for the seed of eternity planted in the soul. The world has our hands, but our soul belongs to Someone Else. Six days a week we seek to dominate the world, on the seventh day we try to dominate the self.[2]

The abundance we have is not our own. Praising this fact, resting in it, and acting with justice for others on behalf of it is at the core of our mission from the God of Abraham, Isaac, Jacob, and Jesus Christ. There are deep links between resisting the cult of needing to work all the time and resisting the seductive

---

[2]Abraham Joshua Heschel, *The Sabbath: Its Meaning for Modern Man* (1951; New York: Farrar, Straus and Giroux, 2005), 13–14.

notion that we deserve all we have—that the one who is in need is someone who has not worked hard enough or is not deserving of abundance. Rest and renewal is testimony, and it is energy for action. To rest in abundance is to rise determined to share abundance, and to combat the structures that deny God's plenty to any of God's children on earth.

And that is perhaps the primary reason why I have come to regard the question, "What will make your heart sing?" as no light and fluffy thing. Indeed, in many respects it is a deeply countercultural question—as countercultural as Sabbath rhythms were and are in the Christian tradition. It is a question that displaces productivity as the measure of effectiveness, even as it recognizes that the most spiritually rooted and joyful pastors also tend to be in a much better position to "produce" excellent ministry—to own our God-given selves as ministers of God's benevolence, sent into the world (ordained or not) to be agents of God's abundance.

Renewal leaves follow the deep logic of the Christian story by locating the worth of pastors, congregations, and the ministry they produce within the economy of God's grace and God's abundance—not in endless "labor." This economy has strange metrics for measuring success—witness Jesus' parable of the laborers in the vineyard! Excellence from the standpoint of heaven is not measured in such earthly metrics as bodies and dollars. It is measured in abiding faithfulness and the cultivation of joy in God. To the extent that sabbaticals can contribute to shared excellence in ministry between pastors and congregations in this way, they are effective in the best way possible.

Conclusion

My hope is that this book has helped your congregation muse about possibilities—how to craft a renewal experience that can be rewarding for the pastor and congregation alike. As you can no doubt tell, I believe that sabbaticals are a powerful tool for renewing pastors, but are so much more so within the context of an entire congregation taking on the opportunity to view the period as one of renewal for the entire congregation.

To reiterate some key points from the book:

1. While pastors are not the only professionals in our society who deserve sabbatical rest, the joys and challenges of pastoral ministry are such that sabbaticals have become common and effective tools for addressing the task of spiritual renewal for pastors and their congregations.

2. If you introduce the idea of renewal leave to the congregation and your encounter resistance or critical questions, do not become defensive; rather, embrace this as a time to have honest conversation about the shared ministry of the pastor and congregation and how this opportunity might be fitted to the particularities of your context.

3. No time spent gaining congregational buy-ins for renewal leaves is wasted; it is one of the most valuable parts of the renewal itself, whether it takes three months or three years.

4. The better the renewal period for the congregation, the better the sabbatical time for the pastor, and vice versa.

From discernment to planning to execution, the pastor and the congregation should undertake this adventure together.

5. Sabbaticals are only profitable for healthy pastors in healthy congregations; burnt-out pastors or congregations in conflict need other kinds of intervention.

6. Pastors should choose activities for their leaves out of joy and not obligation, and be careful not to load the leave with so many activities that it becomes exhausting. And the more extensively the leave is planned, the more room there is for creative spontaneity that enhances, instead of detracting from the renewal goals.

7. Congregations should be creative in the activities that they pursue while the pastor is away; the only activities to be avoided are ones that will results in strategic or operational conversations that are best held after the pastor and congregation are reunited (so that the pastor can be present).

8. Communication between a pastor and a congregation during the leave should be minimal and, ideally, asynchronous (not in real time).

9. Renewal leaves bring us closer to God's mission by reminding us that rest in God's abundance and the desire to share God's abundance with those unjustly deprived of it are deeply intertwined, and that each feed each other.

May your congregation be blessed in its dreaming and in its renewal for God's work in God's beloved world.

Bibliography

Brueggemann, Walter. *Sabbath as Resistance: Saying No to the Culture of Now*. Louisville: Westminster John Knox Press, 2014.

Bullock, Richard, and Richard J. Bruesehoff. *Clergy Renewal: The Alban Guide to Sabbatical Planning*. Herndon, Va.: Alban Institute, 2000.

Dykstra, Craig. "Imagination and the Pastoral Life," available at https://www.religion-online.org/article/imagination-and-the-pastoral-life/.

Haller, Laurie. *Recess: Rediscovering Play and Purpose*. Canton: Cass Community Publishing, 2015.

Heschel, Abraham Joshua. *The Sabbath: Its Meaning for Modern Man*. 1951; New York: Farrar, Straus and Giroux, 2005.

Levine, Robert. *Power Sabbatical: The Break that Makes a Difference*. Findhorn Press, 2007.

Lillyclergyrenewal.org

Louisville-institute.org/programs-grants-and-fellowships/grants/pastoral-study-project/

Muller, Wayne. *Sabbath: Finding Rest, Renewal, and Delight in Our Busy Lives*. New York: Bantam, 1999.

Sevier, Melissa Bane. *Journeying Toward Renewal: A Spiritual Companion for Pastoral Sabbaticals*. Bethesda, Md.: Alban Institute, 2002.

Smith, C. Christopher, and John Pattison. *Slow Church: Cultivating Community in the Patient Way of Jesus*. Downers Grove, Ill.: InterVarsity Press, 2014.